HARSH or HEROIC?

The Middle Ages

SHOCKWAVE
SOCIAL STUDIES

Karen Latchana Kenney

children's press®
An imprint of Scholastic Inc.
NEW YORK • TORONTO • LONDON • AUCKLAND • SYDNEY
MEXICO CITY • NEW DELHI • HONG KONG
DANBURY, CONNECTICUT

Library of Congress Cataloging-in-Publication Data

Kenney, Karen Latchana.
    Harsh or heroic? : the Middle Ages / by Karen Latchana Kenney.
        p. cm. -- (Shockwave)
    Includes index.
    ISBN-10: 0-531-17754-8 (lib. bdg.)
    ISBN-13: 978-0-531-17754-9 (lib. bdg.)
    ISBN-10: 0-531-18794-2 (pbk.)
    ISBN-13: 978-0-531-18794-4 (pbk.)
 1. Middle Ages--Juvenile literature. 2. Europe--Civilization--Juvenile literature.
3. Europe--History--476-1492--Juvenile literature. 4. Europe--Social
conditions--To 1492--Juvenile literature. 5. Civilization, Medieval--Juvenile literature.
I. Title. II. Series.

    D117.K46 2007
    940.1--dc22

2007012245

Published in 2008 by Children's Press, an imprint of Scholastic Inc.,
557 Broadway, New York, New York 10012
www.scholastic.com

08 09 10 11 12 13 14 15 16 17
10 9 8 7 6 5 4 3 2 1

Printed in China through Colorcraft Ltd., Hong Kong

Author: Karen Latchana Kenney
Educational Consultant: Ian Morrison
Editors: Janine Scott and Nadja Embacher
Designer: Emma Alsweiler
Photo Researchers: Jamshed Mistry and Janine Scott

Photographs by: Courtesy of the Medieval Shop, NZ (p. 3); **DK Images** (squire and master,
pp. 20–21); **Getty Images** (plague victim, Joan of Arc, pp. 8–9; nobleman surveying estate,
p. 11; board game, p. 13; trebuchet, gatehouse entrance, p. 15; dining scene, peasant with
crossbow, pp. 18–19; crusaders, p. 23; medieval childbirth, p. 24; woman reading, p. 25; peasants
at market, p. 27); **Hedingham Castle/www.hedinghamcastle.com** (great hall, p. 18); **Jennifer
and Brian Lupton** (teenagers, pp. 30–31); **Photolibrary** (cover; tournament, pp. 8–9; king, p. 11;
peasant's house, manor house, pp. 12–13; lancet window, p. 15; skeleton gibber; pit grill, p. 17;
game animals, p. 19; knight on horseback, p. 20; chapel, p. 23; spinning, p. 25; carpenter's
workshop, helmet, pp. 28–29); **Tranz:** Corbis (p. 1; p. 5; Richard the Lionheart, p. 9; cultivating
fields, pp. 10–11; hunting, p. 13; p. 16; bathroom, p. 16–17; tournament, p. 21; p. 22; illuminated
manuscript, p. 23; lady with maidservant, pp. 24–25; p. 26; market hall, p. 27; categories of craft,
p. 29); Rex Features (garderobe, p. 17); **©Trevor Pearson/Alamy** (pp. 6–7)

All illustrations and other photographs © Weldon Owen Education Inc.

CONTENTS

castle a large, fortified building typical
of medieval Europe

chivalry (*SHIV uhl ree*) the code of behavior that
a medieval knight was expected to follow

Crusades a series of Christian expeditions made
by Europeans between 1096 and 1270 to recapture
the Holy Land (Palestine) from the Muslims

knight (*NITE*) a medieval warrior who wore armor
and fought on horseback with a sword or a long lance

medieval (*med ee EE vuhl*) to do with the Middle Ages

Middle Ages the period in European history from
about 500 A.D. to about 1500 A.D.

moat a deep, wide ditch surrounding a castle,
which is usually filled with water

noble (*NOH buhl*) the upper class in society

For easy reference, see Wordmark on back flap.
For additional vocabulary, see Glossary on page 32.

The word *chivalry* comes
from the French word
chevalerie, which means
"horse soldiery."

The **Middle Ages** covered a period of a thousand years from about 500 A.D. to 1500 A.D. Before the Middle Ages, Europe was ruled by the mighty Roman Empire. However, with the collapse of Roman rule, Europe plunged into a time of turmoil and violent **conquests** as local tribes and rulers tried to invade and steal land from their neighbors. Kings sought to gain power and land. **Knights** who pledged loyalty to their king fought against such invaders.

Emblems for Knights

During the early 1100s, knights began putting an emblem, or coat of arms, on their shields and flags. A coat of arms was a knight's personal signature. Each knight created his own combination of colors, patterns, and symbols. No two knights had the same coat of arms. That way, a knight's followers could recognize him on the battlefield.

SYMBOLS FOR SONS

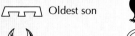	Oldest son		Fourth son
	Second son		Fifth son
	Third son		Sixth son

The Middle Ages were a time of great contrast. Most people were peasants. Their lives were controlled by powerful landowners, called **lords**. Peasants had very few rights. However, toward the end of the Middle Ages, many peasants left the land to work in the growing towns. As trade boomed, a growing class of **merchants** and skilled craftworkers developed. Many became rich and powerful.

Reenactment of a battle

Early Middle Ages 500–1000

☐ **500s**
- Western Europe is divided into many kingdoms after the Roman Empire collapses (about 476).

☐ **900s**
- Western Europe is divided into large estates, which are ruled by lords.
- First castles are made of wood.

High Middle Ages 1000–1300

☐ **1000–1100s**
- Trade flourishes and towns grow.
- Many people move to the towns.

☐ **1100s**
- Castles are now made of stone.
- Knights protect the lords.

Late Middle Ages 1300–1500

☐ **1342–1347**
- About one-third of Europe's people die from a disease called the **plague**.

☐ **1400s**
- The importance of knights declines.

☐ **1500s**
- The importance of castles declines.

HARSH OR HEROIC?

I n a **castle** atop a lofty hill, flags fly from towering turrets. A beautiful lady stands at the balcony of a tall tower. Below, a knight in full armor parades on his horse.

I think italics were used here to help the reader understand that this section is fictional. That's a great way to separate fact and fiction.

This sounds exciting, doesn't it? Well, in the Middle Ages, life was far less colorful than that. Wealth and power lay in the hands of only a few. For most, life was very harsh. Lighting, heating, and sanitation were basic. The threat of disease, war, or **famine** was a daily reality. The average life expectancy was about 30 years. Despite the harsh living conditions, the Middle Ages were later idealized. A knight's life was seen as heroic, helping the weak and poor, and defending his king. He rescued damsels in distress from the tallest towers and fought imaginary, fire-breathing dragons!

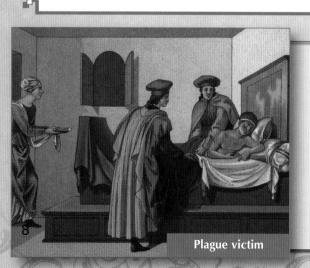

Plague victim

Diseases that are treatable today had harsh and often deadly results in the Middle Ages. Leprosy, an infectious disease, spread to epidemic proportions in Europe during the 1100s and 1200s. Plague killed about 30 million people in Europe and Asia in the mid-1300s. Back then, people didn't know that it was caused by the infected fleas of black rats.

Wars and battles were a harsh reality of life during medieval times. Richard I was king of England from 1189 to 1199. He was known as Richard the Lionheart. His brave manner made him a popular king. He spent many years fighting to regain seized land. He died during a castle **siege**.

There were some heroines during the Middle Ages. Joan of Arc was a French peasant who fought at the head of a French army during the Hundred Years' War. The war started in 1337 and ended in 1453! It spanned the reigns of five English kings and five French kings. Joan of Arc was later accused of witchcraft and was burned at the stake.

THE ORDER OF THINGS

Medieval society was organized into a system that was based on the control and distribution of land. This was called the feudal system. Society was made up of three main groups: the lords, the **clergy**, and the peasants. The lords were powerful landowners who were granted land by the king. In return for land, the lords and their knights promised to serve and defend the king and the country during times of war.

The clergy of the church made up an important group in society. They devoted their lives to the Church. Some were powerful **nobles**. Others were poor and lived in simple cottages near the local church.

The peasants were the largest group of people. They had very few rights. Peasants farmed the lord's land. In return, the lord let them grow food for themselves on a small piece of land. During war, he protected the peasants.

DID YOU KNOW?

There was another group of people between the peasants and the lords. A freeholder didn't live or work on the lord's land, but owned his own land.

Medieval Society
- lords – powerful landowners
- clergy – devoted to church life
- peasants – farmed the lord's land

The peasants were the working class. They labored hard in the fields for the lord. In times of war, they served as soldiers. **Serfs** were the lowest class of peasants.

Medieval kings believed that they had total control over their kingdom and subjects. They managed the land, collected taxes, made laws, and settled disputes among their people.

Medieval nobles promised to serve their king. Sometimes the nobles became so powerful that the king could not control them anymore. Nobles enjoyed special rights and privileges. On their land, they made the rules. They collected taxes for themselves and their king.

SHOCKER

A serf had almost no rights. He had to ask permission to marry, and his children became the lord's property.

11

THE MANOR

In the Middle Ages, most country people lived on a manor. This consisted of a village, the manor house, a church, and surrounding farmland. The manor was owned and governed by a lord. Wealthy lords often owned several manors. The lord and his family lived in a manor house or castle, along with their servants.

The lord appointed several people to run the manor. A steward was the most important. He organized the farmwork and kept the accounts. A bailiff handed out the jobs and ensured that the buildings and tools were in good order. A reeve made sure the peasants worked hard and didn't steal from the lord.

Medieval peasant house

Thatched roof

Stone walls

Wooden fence

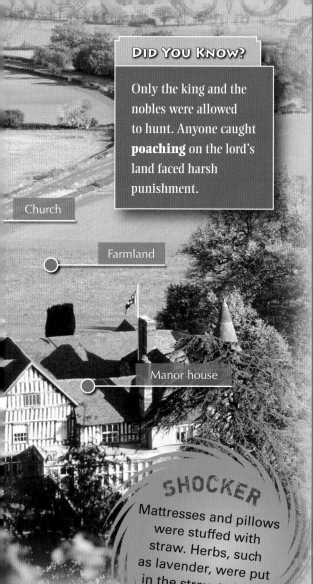

DID YOU KNOW?

Only the king and the nobles were allowed to hunt. Anyone caught **poaching** on the lord's land faced harsh punishment.

Church

Farmland

Manor house

SHOCKER

Mattresses and pillows were stuffed with straw. Herbs, such as lavender, were put in the straw to keep the bugs away.

Peasants lived in simple cottages. The outside walls were often made from wattle and daub. Wattle was made from thin pieces of interwoven wood. Daub consisted of dung, straw, and clay. Often a cottage had only two rooms. The furniture was basic. A thatched roof kept the rain out of the cottage. A stone hearth in the main room helped keep the cottage warm. However, peasant cottages didn't have chimneys!

After taking care of the manor business, the lord, **lady**, and their noble friends enjoyed many leisure activities. Inside, they played cards and board games, such as chess. They listened to storytellers, **jesters**, and musicians.

Outdoors, nobles and kings went hunting and hawking. Hawking was a favorite sport. They used trained hawks, eagles, or falcons to hunt and catch small animals, such as rabbits, hares, and ducks.

13

MY HOME, MY CASTLE

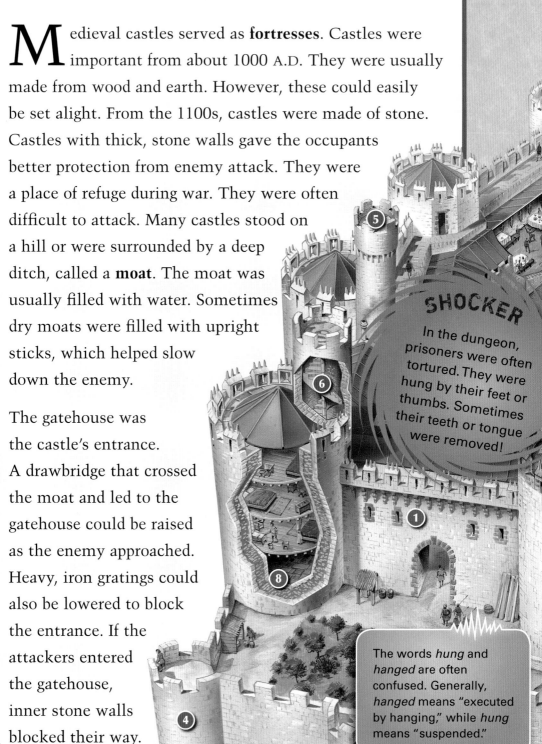

Medieval castles served as **fortresses**. Castles were important from about 1000 A.D. They were usually made from wood and earth. However, these could easily be set alight. From the 1100s, castles were made of stone. Castles with thick, stone walls gave the occupants better protection from enemy attack. They were a place of refuge during war. They were often difficult to attack. Many castles stood on a hill or were surrounded by a deep ditch, called a **moat**. The moat was usually filled with water. Sometimes dry moats were filled with upright sticks, which helped slow down the enemy.

The gatehouse was the castle's entrance. A drawbridge that crossed the moat and led to the gatehouse could be raised as the enemy approached. Heavy, iron gratings could also be lowered to block the entrance. If the attackers entered the gatehouse, inner stone walls blocked their way.

SHOCKER

In the dungeon, prisoners were often tortured. They were hung by their feet or thumbs. Sometimes their teeth or tongue were removed!

The words *hung* and *hanged* are often confused. Generally, *hanged* means "executed by hanging," while *hung* means "suspended."

Some gatehouses had murder holes in the ceilings. People defending the castle threw boiling water, boiling **pitch**, or hot sand through these holes onto the enemy below.

Sling pouch for missile

Rope to pull arm down

A catapult machine, known as a trebuchet, helped the enemy knock holes in castle walls. A large, wooden pivoting arm hurled missiles such as stone balls. The balls weighed up to 200 pounds.

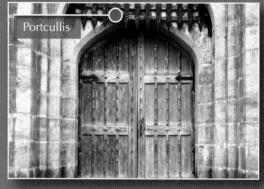

Portcullis

The gatehouse entrance was heavily protected. If the attackers managed to cross the drawbridge, they were faced with an iron grating, called a portcullis, which could be lowered. There were also heavy wooden doors.

1. **Lancet window** a narrow window that let light and air in. It was easy to shoot out of, but difficult to shoot into!

2. **Natural defense** a hill or seawall

3. **Drawbridge** a wooden bridge that could be lifted up or pulled back

4. **Outside wall** a high stone wall that could be as much as 20 feet thick

5. **Watchtower** the highest point of the castle to look out for enemy attack

6. **Spiral staircase** a staircase that wound up and around to the right. This made it hard for an enemy running up, as a knight usually held his sword in his right hand.

7. **Gatehouse** an entrance protected by a heavy, iron grating, called a portcullis

8. **Dungeon** a prison where the enemy was kept and sometimes tortured

Lancet windows often had a round area in the narrow opening. This allowed cannon balls to be fired out of them.

Castles were family homes too. They were usually made from stone, so they could be cold and dark. In early castles, fires were built in the middle of the stone floor of the **great hall**, which was the heart of the castle. This provided the main part of the castle with its heating. Torches and candles provided the lighting. By the late 1100s, the great hall was heated by fireplaces.

Fireplaces in private rooms, or chambers, were more common by the 1200s. Medieval beds had heavy curtains around them. There was a practical reason for this. They were drawn to keep out cold drafts. Often the castle floors were covered with rushes or rush matting. The rushes needed to be changed regularly. Sometimes herbs were scattered on the floor too. As people walked on the floor, the herbs released a pleasant, refreshing smell.

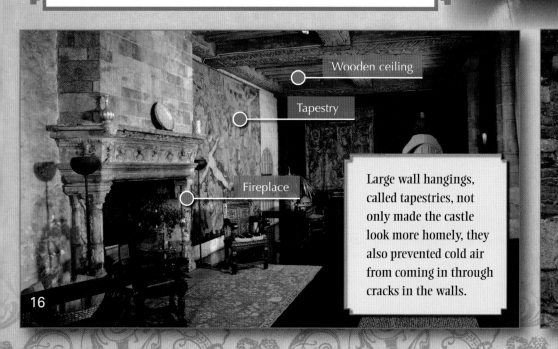

Wooden ceiling

Tapestry

Fireplace

Large wall hangings, called tapestries, not only made the castle look more homely, they also prevented cold air from coming in through cracks in the walls.

Sometimes there was a toilet called a garderobe inside the castle. It was located next to the lord's private chambers. The human waste went down a long chute and out through a hole in the outer castle wall. The waste dropped into pits or even the moat!

One place in the castle was very dark and damp – the dungeon! There prisoners might be locked in an iron cage, called a gibbet (above). They were left to starve to death. Some prisoners were thrown into pits under the floor (below).

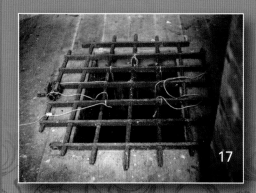

17

One of the warmest parts of the castle was the kitchen. Great feasts for the lord and his guests were prepared by many servants. During a siege, however, food could become scarce. The enemy would try to cut off the castle's supplies of water and food in order to make the occupants surrender.

Near the kitchen was the great hall. There the lord and lady entertained guests. The most important guests sat on a raised platform, or dais (*DAY uhss*). This "high table" was served first. The more important the person was, the closer he or she sat to the lord. The less important guests sat at the "low tables."

I wasn't sure what *siege* meant, but I continued reading and figured it out. Then I checked it in the glossary just to make sure. I often find reading on to be helpful when I am unsure.

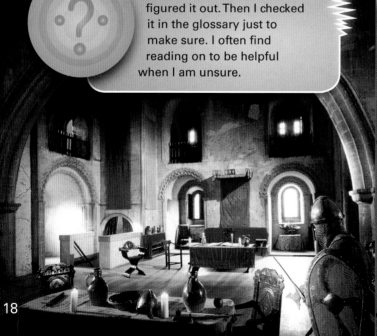

During the day, the lord conducted his business in the great hall. He collected taxes and rents. He settled disputes and meted out punishment for crimes.

Many servants helped with the running of the castle. Wealthy households often had hundreds of servants. Usually boys served the food.

People in the Middle Ages hunted for their meat with bows or crossbows (above). They hunted for rabbits, pheasants, and deer. They even ate swans and blackbirds. The dead animals hung in the kitchen.

Jobs for Royal Servants

- Keeper of the greyhounds
- Keeper of the king's bow
- Keeper of the royal bed
- Keeper of the tents
- Taster of the king's food

19

Knights in Armor

Knights were the brave soldiers of medieval society. They were usually from noble families. They lived by a set of rules called the code of **chivalry**.

A young noble boy who wanted to become a knight was sent to live in another noble household at age seven. Called a page, he was taught how to use weapons, hunt, and ride horses. He was also taught chess. This game helped the page learn the skills and strategies needed for war. At age fifteen, he became a squire, which was his master's personal servant. He trained to be a horse soldier. He rode into battle alongside his master. A squire became a knight when he was twenty-one years old.

Squire

SHOCKER
In the 1300s, a suit of armor weighed about 80 pounds. It was so heavy that a knight had to be lifted onto his horse. If he fell off, he needed help to get up.

The tools that a knight needed were a horse, a suit of armor, and weapons. Sometimes a knight's horse wore armor too.

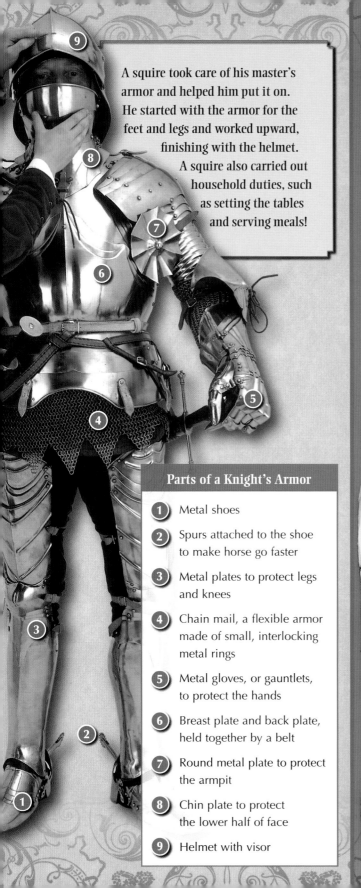

A squire took care of his master's armor and helped him put it on. He started with the armor for the feet and legs and worked upward, finishing with the helmet. A squire also carried out household duties, such as setting the tables and serving meals!

During times of peace, knights took part in mock battles. However, these tournaments could be just as deadly and dangerous as battle. Many knights were wounded or killed in these events.

Parts of a Knight's Armor

1. Metal shoes
2. Spurs attached to the shoe to make horse go faster
3. Metal plates to protect legs and knees
4. Chain mail, a flexible armor made of small, interlocking metal rings
5. Metal gloves, or gauntlets, to protect the hands
6. Breast plate and back plate, held together by a belt
7. Round metal plate to protect the armpit
8. Chin plate to protect the lower half of face
9. Helmet with visor

Code of Chivalry

- Be gentle toward the weak.
- Give to the poor.
- Protect women and children.
- Be brave.
- Defend your personal honor and religion.
- Be humble.
- Be generous.
- Be loyal and true to your word.

THE CHURCH

During the Middle Ages, **Christianity** spread across Europe. The Catholic Church was the Christian religion of medieval Europe. The Church was a very powerful and wealthy **institution**. It was governed by its own set of rules. The Pope was the head of the Church. The Church was also a big part of ordinary people's lives. People went to church on Sundays. They were married in churches and buried in the church grounds.

Many medieval men and women led religious lives. They lived as monks in **monasteries** or as nuns in **convents**. The members of these religious communities devoted their time to reading, praying, and caring for the sick, poor, and elderly. They attended about seven church services a day. Nuns, unlike most medieval women, were able to study and teach.

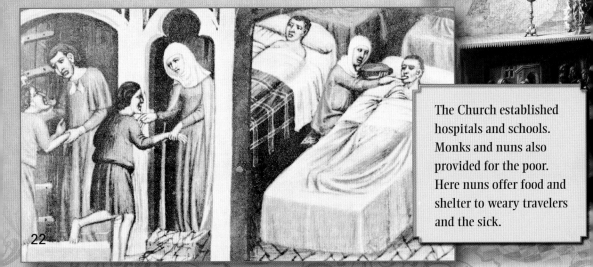

The Church established hospitals and schools. Monks and nuns also provided for the poor. Here nuns offer food and shelter to weary travelers and the sick.

Many castles had a small chapel. It was usually near the lord's chamber. Each morning, a church service was held by a priest for the lord and lady.

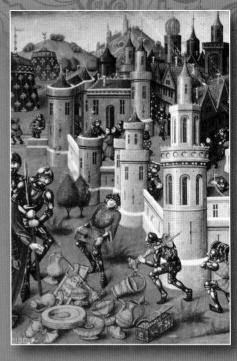

During the Middle Ages, there was a series of religious wars called the **Crusades**. Crusaders were knights from western Europe who tried to recapture the Holy Land (Palestine) from the **Muslims**. Eight expeditions took place between 1096 and 1270.

DID YOU KNOW?

By the end of the Middle Ages, nearly every town and village in Europe had at least one church. No other building was allowed to be built higher than the church.

In the monasteries, monks copied books by hand. Some books were beautifully decorated, or illuminated, with **gold leaf**. By 1440, printing machines with movable type sped up the production of books.

23

MEDIEVAL WOMEN

A peasant woman in the Middle Ages was expected to marry, have children, work alongside her husband in the fields, and feed and clothe her family. To survive, she usually needed to marry. She could marry as young as twelve, with her parents' permission. She may have given birth to many children, of whom only a few survived. Girls were taught by their mothers to cook, spin wool into yarn, and weave.

Girls from noble families were often taught how to read and write, do embroidery, sing, and play an instrument. A noble girl's marriage was usually arranged by her family in order to gain more land and power. Sometimes girls were legally engaged, or betrothed, in childhood. A noblewoman ran the household and organized the servants. If her husband was at war, she ran the manor, collected rents, and even helped defend the manor against attack.

Giving birth could be dangerous for medieval women. Poor hygiene and medical knowledge often resulted in the mother, the baby, or even both dying during childbirth.

Medieval Women	Modern Women
• expected to marry	• can remain unmarried
• expected to have many children	• can choose to have children
• few job opportunities	• many more job opportunities
• childbirth very dangerous	• childbirth much less dangerous

Books were important to medieval noblewomen. Sometimes they left books to other noblewomen when they died. Wealthy girls were often taught to read by tutors.

Noble girls as young as seven were often sent to live with wealthier noble families to be maids. The lady of the manor had ladies-in-waiting, who were her friends and companions. Her maidservants took care of her.

Ordinary women had to make their family's clothes. They brushed the wool with wire combs. Then they spun the fibers and wove them into cloth. Some unmarried women did this for a living. They were called spinsters. Today, *spinster* still means "unmarried woman."

25

In the Town

During the 1000s and 1100s, many peasants moved from the countryside to the towns. Some ran away from the manor and the controlling lord. Serfs were able to obtain their freedom by working for one year and one day in a town. With the development of towns and trade came the beginning of a new class of professionals, such as merchants, bankers, and master craftworkers.

A medieval town was often surrounded by walls that protected the townspeople. However, the walls also caused overcrowding, as the town couldn't spread out into the surrounding countryside. The houses in these walled towns had to be built closely together due to limited space. They were built up, rather than out. Some buildings were up to six stories high. Fire was a real danger in medieval towns. People used torches and candles for lighting. Houses were often made of wood, so fire spread rapidly in the narrow streets.

Don't I feel silly. I misread the word *peasants*. I thought it said *presents*! As I kept reading, it got really confusing. So I went back and reread the first sentence again. That nearly always does the trick.

Carcassonne, France

This market hall is two stories high. The upper floor was used as a chamber for the town council. The ground floor contained the town jail.

Market hall

Shops

This three-story, fifteenth-century building (opposite the market hall) had two shops. The shops were on the ground floor. The shopkeeper lived in the two stories above.

SHOCKER

In medieval towns, people often threw their garbage and bodily waste out their windows and into the streets!

Markets were often held once a week in big towns. Peasants from the surrounding farmland sold their fresh produce, such as eggs, cheese, meat, fruit, and vegetables.

In the town, craftworkers made many everyday items by hand. Expert craftworkers were called masters. A master passed on his skills to an **apprentice**, who had to work for as long as seven years to become a journeyman. To become a master, the journeyman would make a product or "masterpiece," which was judged by the masters of his trade.

Craftworkers organized themselves into associations, or guilds (*GILDS*), of workers with common skills. The guilds controlled wages, working hours, work standards, prices, and even the amount of production. Craftworkers paid fees to become guild members. Women couldn't belong to most guilds. Some guilds were rich and powerful. They helped craftworkers who couldn't work due to old age or illness.

SHOCKER
The executioner had such a low status that no woman wanted to be his wife. A female criminal could receive a pardon if she agreed to marry the executioner!

Making Chain Mail

1. Metal wire is wound around a bar. This makes a coil.

2. Each circle of the coil is cut off, creating a link.

3. Each link is forced through a narrow space. This forces the ends to overlap.

4. More links are threaded through the first link. They are hammered closed.

Craftworkers who made armor belonged to the Armorers' Guild. An armorer also made or repaired chain mail and weapons.

A master's wife and children sometimes helped in the workshop. Often a son would become his father's apprentice.

Odd Medieval Jobs

Barber: Barbers cut hair. They also performed surgery and extracted teeth!

Fuller: Fullers washed newly woven woolen cloth by trampling on it in a vat of stale urine for many hours.

Gong Farmer: Before flush toilets were invented, gong farmers removed "night soil" from the toilets. They worked only at night.

TAILOR

Tailors made clothes for wealthy people. Peasants made and repaired their own clothes.

BAKER

Bakers were kept busy in most medieval cities. They mostly baked whole-grain breads.

BLACKSMITH

Blacksmiths made wagon wheels, horseshoes, and chains for drawbridges and for prisoners.

SHOEMAKER

Shoemakers made leather shoes and boots by hand. Leather from Spain was highly prized.

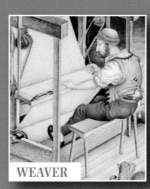

WEAVER

Weavers wove fleece into cloth. Different guilds cleaned, brushed, trimmed, or dyed the cloth.

CLOCKMAKER

Clockmakers were just starting out in the Middle Ages. It is believed the first clocks were made in the late 1200s.

In the Middle Ages, craft guilds were associations of skilled workers that were set up to protect workers' rights. Their aim was to establish better conditions for their members. They set reasonable wages and prices. Today, labor unions are similar to early guilds. They work to improve the wages, hours, and working conditions of their members. They also help settle disputes between workers and their employers.

WHAT DO YOU THINK?

Should all workers join a labor union?

PRO

I think it is a good idea. A labor union looks out for its members. Individual workers may be afraid of getting fired for speaking up. A collective voice has much greater strength. An employer is more likely to take notice of a group.

Labor unions in the United States were first established in the early 1800s. The Industrial Revolution brought about many major changes in the way workers were treated. The factory machines never stopped, so workers had to work long hours, up to 14 hours a day. They were paid very low wages. By joining a labor union, workers found they had more power as a group than as an individual.

CON

Every worker should have the right to choose whether to be part of a labor union. Some people may not agree with the union's aims. Not all workers in the same field have the same abilities. An employee may prefer that his or her employer reward workers individually.

Go to **www.geocities.com/ elangoc/medieval/careers. html** to learn more about craft guilds in the Middle Ages.

apprentice (*uh PREN tiss*) a person who learns a trade by working with a skilled person

Christianity (*kriss chee AN uh tee*) a religion based on the teachings of Jesus

clergy (*KLUR jee*) a group of people trained to perform religious duties in a Christian church

conquest (*KON kwest*) the action of conquering or gaining territory

convent (*KON vent*) a place where nuns live and study religion

famine an extreme shortage of food

fortress a place that is strengthened against attack

gold leaf gold that has been beaten into a thin sheet

great hall the large room in a castle, used for business and feasting

institution (*in stuh TOO shuhn*) a large organization formed for a religious, educational, or social purpose

jester (*JES tur*) an entertainer in the Middle Ages

lady a woman of noble rank

lord a man of noble rank

merchant a person who sells goods at a market

monastery (*MON uh ster ee*) a place where monks live and study religion

Muslim a person who believes in the teachings of the Prophet Muhammad (570–632 A.D.)

pitch a sticky resin that is the sap of conifers

plague (*PLAYG*) a contagious disease caused by bacteria that spreads quickly and causes death

poach (*POHCH*) to hunt animals without permission

serf (*SURF*) a peasant who served and was owned by the lord of the manor

siege (*SEEJ*) a long, drawn-out attack on a city, town, or castle